PHILIP H. PFATTEICHER

FORETASTE OF·THE FEAST TO·COME

Devotions on Holy Communion

 **AUGSBURG** Publishing House • Minneapolis

FORETASTE OF THE FEAST TO COME
Devotions on Holy Communion

Copyright © 1987 Augsburg Publishing House

Scripture quotations except from the Psalms, and translations by the author from the original languages, are from the Revised Standard Version of the Bible, copyright 1946, 1952, and 1971 by the Division of Christian Education of the National Council of Churches.

Library of Congress Cataloging-in-Publication Data

Pfatteicher, Philip H.
    FORETASTE OF THE FEAST TO COME: devotions on Holy Communion
  Philip H. Pfatteicher.
      p. cm.
    ISBN 0-8066-2283-0
    1. Lord's Supper—Prayer-books and devotions—English.
  2. Lutheran Church—Prayer-books and devotions—English. I. Title.
  BX8073.P44   1987   87-15327
  264'.36—dc19   CIP

Manufactured in the U.S.A.   APH 10-2357

1 2 3 4 5 6 7 8 9 0 1 2 3 4 5 6 7 8 9

for Linda
Sarah
Carolyn
Carl

HOLY COMMUNION

The Lord's Supper is a meal that the followers of Jesus share with him and with one another. Such eating and drinking binds them together with each other and with him in Holy Communion. The sacred meal, which through the ages has been the center of Christian worship, keeps alive the memory of the saving acts that God has done in history and makes them live again in the present.

A traditional antiphon from Vespers praises Holy Communion, exclaiming in wonder and admiration:

O sacred feast,
in which Christ is received,
the memorial of his passion is celebrated anew,
our souls are filled with grace,
and we are given a pledge of the glory
which is to come.

Holy Communion gathers and gives shape to the past, while it points its celebrants always forward.

The abounding richness of this feast requires careful preparation by those who intend to share in it if its meanings are to be understood and loved and received with gladness. Moreover, as by our faith and devotion we prepare for Holy Communion, so by our reception of Holy Communion we prepare for the feast to come.

The Church is the place in which today Christ still receives sinners and eats with them.

—Bishop Bo Giertz

In order to strengthen and encourage us . . . God gives us this sacrament, as much as to say, "Look, many kinds of sin are assailing you; take this sign by which I give you my pledge that this sin is assailing not only you, but also my Son, Christ, and all his saints in heaven and on earth. Therefore take heart and be bold. You are not fighting alone. Great help and support are all around you.

This fellowship is two-fold; on the one hand we partake of Christ and all saints; on the other hand we permit all Christians to be partakers of us, in whatever way they and we are able. Thus, by means of this sacrament, all self-seeking love is rooted out and gives place to that which seeks the common good of all; and through the change wrought by love there is one bread, one drink, one body, one community. This is the true unity of Christian brethren.

—Martin Luther

PREPARE

Our Minds,
Our Hearts

Preparation before Holy Communion

Antiphon   You spread a table before me in the
             presence of those who trouble me;
                  you have anointed my head with oil,
                  and my cup is running over.

(Ps. 23:5)

Psalm 27

The Lord is my light and my salvation;
whom then shall I fear?
     The Lord is the strength of my life;
     of whom then shall I be afraid?
When evildoers came upon me
to eat up my flesh,
     it was they, my foes and
     my adversaries, who stumbled and fell.
Though an army
should encamp against me,
     yet my heart shall not be afraid;
and though war
should rise up against me,
     yet will I put my trust in him.
One thing have I asked of the Lord;
one thing I seek;
     that I may dwell

in the house of the Lord
all the days of my life;
to behold the fair beauty of the Lord
and to seek him in his temple.
For in the day of trouble
he shall keep me safe in his shelter;
he shall hide me
in the secrecy of his dwelling
and set me high upon a rock.
Even now he lifts up my head
above my enemies round about me.
Therefore I will offer in his dwelling
an oblation
with sounds of great gladness;
I will sing
and make music to the Lord.
Hearken to my voice, O Lord,
when I call;
have mercy on me and answer me.
You speak in my heart and say,
"Seek my face."
Your face, Lord, will I seek.
Hide not your face from me,
nor turn away your servant
in displeasure.
You have been my helper;

cast me not away;
do not forsake me,
O God of my salvation.
Though my father and my mother
forsake me,
the Lord will sustain me.
Show me your way, O Lord;
lead me on a level path,
because of my enemies.
Deliver me not
into the hand of my adversaries,
for false witnesses
have risen up against me,
and also those who speak malice.
What if I had not believed that I
should see the goodness of the Lord
in the land of the living!
Oh, tarry and await the Lord's pleasure;
be strong,
and he shall comfort your heart;
wait patiently for the Lord.

OR

Psalm 84

How dear to me is your dwelling,
O Lord of hosts!
  My soul has a desire and longing
  for the courts of the Lord;
  my heart and my flesh rejoice
  in the living God.
The sparrow has found her a house
and the swallow a nest
where she may lay her young,
  by the side of your altars,
  O Lord of hosts,
  my King and my God.
Happy are they
who dwell in your house!
  They will always be praising you.
Happy are the people
whose strength is in you,
  whose hearts are set
  on the pilgrims' way.
Those who go
through the desolate valley
will find it a place of springs,
  for the early rains have covered it
  with pools of water.

They will climb from height to height,
   and the God of gods
   will reveal himself in Zion.
Lord God of hosts, hear my prayer,
   hearken, O God of Jacob.
Behold our defender, O God;
   and look upon the face
   of your anointed.
For one day in your courts
is better than a thousand
in my own room,
   and to stand at the threshold
   of the house of my God than
   to dwell in the tents of the wicked.
For the Lord God
is both sun and shield;
   he will give grace and glory;
no good thing will the Lord withhold
   from those who walk with integrity.
O Lord of hosts,
   happy are they
   who put their trust in you!

Antiphon   You spread a table before me in the
presence of those who trouble me;
   you have anointed my head with oil,
   and my cup is running over.

During Advent and Lent this psalm is used:

Antiphon Remember not our past sins;
let your compassion be swift to meet us;
for we have been brought very low.

(Ps. 79:8)

Psalm 130

Out of the depths
have I called to you, O Lord;
Lord, hear my voice,
    let your ears consider well
    the voice of my supplication.
If you, Lord,
were to note what is done amiss,
    O Lord, who could stand?
For there is forgiveness with you,
    therefore you shall be feared.
I wait for the Lord;
my soul waits for him,
    in his word is my hope.
My soul waits for the Lord,
more than watchmen for the morning,
    more than watchmen
    for the morning.

O Israel, wait for the Lord,
    for with the Lord there is mercy;
with him
there is plenteous redemption,
    and he shall redeem Israel
    from all their sins.

Antiphon   Remember not our past sins;
            let your compassion be swift to meet us;
                for we have been brought very low.

Lord have mercy.
Christ have mercy.
Lord have mercy.

✠

Lord, be merciful to me;
   heal me, for I have sinned against you (Ps. 41:4).
Return, O Lord; how long will you tarry?
   Be gracious to your servants (Ps. 90:13).
Have mercy on me, O God,
   I will put my trust in you (Ps. 56:1,3).
Let your priests be clothed with righteousness;
   let your faithful people sing with joy (Ps. 132:9).
Cleanse me from my secret faults.
   Above all, keep your servant from presumptuous
   sins (Ps. 19:12-13).
Lord, hear my prayer,
   and let my cry come before you (Ps. 102:1).

✠

Most gracious God, incline your merciful ears to
our prayers and enlighten our hearts by the grace of
your Holy Spirit, that we may approach your Holy
Mysteries with believing hearts and love you with
an everlasting love.

✠

O Lord, may the Counsellor who proceeds from you
illumine our minds and, as your Son promised,
lead us into all truth.

✠

O Lord, may the power of the Holy Spirit be with us
to cleanse and purge our hearts
and to defend us against all adversities.

✠

Lord God,
you taught the hearts of your faithful people
by sending them the light of your Holy Spirit.
Grant that we, by your Spirit,
may have a right judgment in all things
and evermore rejoice in his holy counsel;
through your Son, Jesus Christ our Lord.

✠

Cleanse our consciences, O Lord, by your coming,
that your Son our Lord Jesus Christ when he appears
may find in us a dwelling place prepared for himself;
through the same your Son Jesus Christ our Lord,
who lives and reigns with you and the Holy Spirit,
one God, now and forever.

✠

A prayer of Thomas Aquinas

Almighty and everlasting God,
behold I draw near to the sacrament of your only Son
our Lord Jesus Christ.

As one sick, I come to the Physician of life;
as unclean, to the Fountain of mercy;
as blind, to the Light of eternal splendor;
as poor and needy, to the Lord of heaven and earth;
as naked, to the King of glory;
a lost sheep, to the Good Shepherd;
a fallen creature to its Creator;
desolate, to the Comforter;
sorrowful, to the Pitier;
guilty, to the Bestower of pardon;
sinful, to the Justifier;
hardened, to the Giver of grace.

Therefore in your boundless mercy, Lord, I implore
you

to heal my sickness,
wash my defilement,
enlighten my blindness,
enrich my poverty,
clothe my nakedness.

Then shall I dare to receive the Bread of Angels,
    the King of kings and Lord of lords,
    with reverence and fear,
    contrition and love,
    faith and purity,
    devotion and humility.
Grant that I may so receive the Body of your Son
Jesus Christ
    which he took from the Virgin Mary
    that I may be incorporated into his mystical body
    and be numbered among his people.
Most loving Father, grant that your beloved Son,
    whom I now receive hidden in bread and wine,
    I may at last behold face to face;
        for he lives and reigns with you and the Holy
        Spirit, one God,
        now and forever.

Additional Prayers of Preparation

These prayers may be said one by one on the days of the week preceding the Communion, beginning on Monday.

Eternal God,
    the light of the minds that know you,
    the joy of the hearts that love you,
    the strength of the wills that serve you;
grant us so to know you that we may truly love you,
    so to love you that we may freely serve you;
        to the glory of your holy name.

✛

Jesus, Master,
come and meet us while we walk in the way
and long to reach the heavenly country,
so that, following your light,
we may keep the way of righteousness and justice and,
while you who are the Way, the Truth, and the Life
    are shining within us,
we may never wander away into the darkness
    of this world's night.

✛

Come, Lord Jesus, in the fullness of your grace,
and dwell in the hearts of your servants;

that, adoring you by faith,
we may receive you with joy,
and with love and thankfulness abide in you,
  our Guide,
  the Bread of Pilgrims,
  our Companion on the Way.

✠

O Lord, forgive the sins of your servants.
Help us banish from our minds all disunion and strife;
cleansing our spirits from all anger and malice.
Let us join in the Holy Mysteries
  with unity and harmony of mind
  and at peace with one another.

✠

Lord God of all the ages,
open our eyes
to see your hand at work in the world about us.
Deliver us from the presumption
  of coming to this table for solace only, and not for
  strength;
    for pardon only, and not for renewal.
Let the grace of this Holy Communion make us one
body, one spirit,
  that we may worthily serve the world in your name.

✠

Come, Lord Jesus, and stand among us
as you once stood among your disciples.

As watchmen wait for the morning,
so do we wait for you, O Christ.
Come with the dawning of the day
and reveal yourself to us in the breaking of the bread,
as once you revealed yourself to your disciples.

Preparation of the Ministers
for the Service of God

Holy is the holy Father,
Holy is the holy Son,
Holy is the life-creating holy Spirit.
Glory to the Father, and to the Son,
and to the Holy Spirit;
and upon us, weak and sinful, be mercy and grace,
now and forever.

> Lord have mercy.
> Christ have mercy.
> Lord have mercy.

Into your house, O God, we have entered,
your holy vessels we have prepared,
the garments of purity put on.
To your sanctuary we come to minister
before your whole Church on earth
and the holy company of the redeemed,
to serve at your altar
and to worship in your presence,
O Christ our God forever.

I will wash my hands in innocence, O Lord,
   that I may go in procession round your altar
singing aloud a song of thanksgiving
   and recounting all your wonderful deeds.
Lord, I love the house in which you dwell
   and the place where your glory abides.

(Ps. 26:6-8)

☩

Cleanse us wholly, O Lord,
making us pure temples
fit for the service of your glory
and for the praise of your holy name,
O Lord our God forever.

☩

O pure and spotless Lamb,
you offered to the Father an acceptable offering
for the redemption of the whole world.
Grant that we may offer ourselves to you
as living sacrifices,
like unto your sacrifice which was for us,
O Christ our God forever.

☩

O Lord, make us worthy to offer to you
sacrifices of praise
   as a sweet-smelling savor
all our thoughts and words and deeds
   in pure longing after you;
and so without stain to appear before you
   all the days of our life,
O Father, Son, and Holy Spirit, forever.

Holy is the holy Father,
Holy is the holy Son,
Holy is the life-creating holy Spirit.
Glory to the Father, and to the Son,
and to the Holy Spirit;
and upon us, weak and sinful, be mercy and grace,
now and forever.

Let Us Draw Near

Echoes of Baptism resound throughout the celebration of the Holy Communion, for these two sacraments shape the Christian life. Baptism, by which we are born anew and in which our Christian life begins, gives us confidence to approach the altar of God.

Purge me from my sin, and I shall be pure;
    wash me, and I shall be clean indeed (Ps. 51:8).
Wash me through and through from my wickedness,
    and cleanse me from my sin (Ps. 51:2).
Show us your mercy, O Lord,
    and grant us your salvation (Ps. 85:7).
Lord, hear my prayer,
    and let my cry come before you (Ps. 102:1).

✠

Holy Lord, almighty Father, everlasting God,
hear our prayer and send your holy angel from heaven
to guard, protect, visit, and defend all those
who assemble together in this house;
through Jesus Christ our Lord.

✠

Therefore . . . since we have confidence to enter the sanctuary by the blood of Jesus, by the new and living way which he opened for us through the curtain, that is, through his flesh, and since we have a great high priest over the house of God, let us draw near with a true heart in full assurance of faith, with our hearts sprinkled clean from an evil conscience and our bodies washed with pure water.

(Heb. 10:19-21)

I was glad when they said to me,
"Let us go to the house of the Lord."

(Ps. 122:1)

CELEBRATE

*Hear the Word,
Share the Feast*

The Entrance of the Ministers

Whenever we worship, the biblical stories come alive. The past lives again in us, and we are drawn on to the goal of all creation.

The entrance of the ministers at the beginning of the service, like all Christian ritual processions, is a dramatic portrayal of the pilgrim church, passing through this world toward that which is to come. We go in search of our true homeland in that heavenly country which God has prepared for his people (see Heb. 11:13-16). We follow in the company of Abraham, the model for all the faithful who set out boldly in search of spiritual truth.

At the entrance we also portray the hope of the prophet's vision of the nations streaming up the mountain of God to worship him in his temple (see Mic. 4:1-4 and Isa. 2:2-4).

Send out your light and your truth
that they may lead me,
   and bring me to your holy hill and to your dwelling;
that I may go to the altar of God,
   to the God of my joy and gladness.

(Ps. 43:3-4)

The Reading and Preaching of the Holy Scripture

Grant, O Lord, that we may be illumined by him
who is the Light,
    directed by him who is the Way,
    corrected by him who is the Truth,
    and quickened by him who is the Life
and who now lives and reigns with you and the
    Holy Spirit, one God,
    now and forever.

                    Wisdom! Let us attend.

God's Word is proclaimed to his people through *a
reading from the Original Covenant,* telling of God's
mighty deeds among his people:

The steadfast love of the Lord never ceases,
    his mercies never come to an end;
they are new every morning (Lam. 3:22-23a).

During Easter, the First Lesson is taken from the Book
of the Acts of the Apostles.

God's Word is proclaimed through *a reading from
the Apostle,* read today in the Christian community
as the Apostle's letters were originally read in the
churches:

I adjure you by the Lord that this letter be read to all the brethren (1 Thess. 5:27).

So then . . . stand firm and hold to the traditions which you were taught by us, either by word of mouth or by letter (2 Thess. 2:15).

God's Word is proclaimed through *a reading from the Gospel of our Lord Jesus Christ,* welcomed by the Alleluia and surrounded before and after by the Gospel acclamations. We pass from the words of the servants of God to the words of our Lord himself, and the ministry of the Word comes to its climax as we stand to listen to Christ speaking to his people now. We address our responses to him as to one actually present:

When the Gospel is read, let all the presbyters and all the deacons and all the people stand very quietly to hear the words of the King of kings.

God's Word is proclaimed through *a statement in the language of today—the sermon.* The preacher witnesses in contemporary terms to the truth of the ancient Scriptures, delivering the sermon to the congregation, and they in turn deliver it to the world:

Grant, O Lord, that your Word alone
may be spoken
    and that your Word alone may be heard.

The Prayers of Intercession

The liturgy of the Word of God is concluded with the prayers of the people who make intercession for all and who give thanks on behalf of all. By these prayers we reach out our arms to embrace the concerns of all humanity.

Remember all your creation for good, O Lord,
Visit the world with your compassion,
and have mercy on all.

The Offering of Our Gifts

The focus of attention in the Service now moves from the reading desk to the altar table, from the place of reading and preaching to the place of the meal.

In preparation, we offer to God for God's use everything we have, for God's work in us cannot be effective until the ordinary material of our lives, just as it is, is turned over entirely to God. In the bread and wine and money we offer samples of this world with all its sin upon it. We offer all that is necessary for life and all that makes it glad; we spread before God also our corruption of God's good gifts. We give to God the grain and the grapes which God has provided and as human labor and commercial production have worked upon them. The gifts stand not only for what God has given us; they also represent what we have made of God's gifts—the abundance and poverty, generosity and greed, moderation and excess.

In this sacrament, God, who gave us everything we have to offer, takes our offered gifts and our lives and blesses them and gives them back to us washed and transformed and made new, so that we may go confidently into the world to be God's people, doing the works of Christ.

I appeal to you therefore . . . by the mercies of God, to present your bodies as a living sacrifice, holy and acceptable to God, which is your spiritual worship. Do not be conformed to this world but be transformed by the renewal of your mind, that you may prove what is the will of God, what is good and acceptable and perfect.

(Rom. 12:1-2)

Through [Jesus Christ] then let us continually offer up a sacrifice of praise to God, that is, the fruit of lips that acknowledge his name. Do not neglect to do good and to share what you have, for such sacrifices are pleasing to God.

(Heb. 13:15-16)

The Great Thanksgiving

In this central prayer of the whole service we commemorate with high thanksgiving our perfect redemption through the mighty work of God in Christ, and we pray that he will come among us now to transform our lives through his life.

The solemn proclamation of thanksgiving begins with the very ancient dialog which lifts us to take our share, as part of the Church Triumphant, in the ceaseless worship of the citizens of heaven:

After this I looked, and lo, in heaven an open door! And the first voice, which I had heard speaking to me like a trumpet, said, "Come up hither."

Behold, a great multitude which no one could number,
from every nation, from all tribes and peoples and tongues, standing before the throne and before the Lamb.

And all the angels fell on their faces before the throne and worshiped God.
And day and night they never cease to sing,
  'Holy, holy, holy, is the Lord God Almighty,
  who was and is and is to come!'

(Rev. 4:1; 7:9,11; 4:8)

Let us who mystically represent the Cherubim
   in singing the thrice-holy hymn
      to the life-giving Trinity
now lay aside all earthly care
   so that we may welcome the King of all
      who comes escorted by invisible hosts of angels.
Alleluia. Alleluia. Alleluia.

Before the glorious throne of your Kingdom,
   the unattainable seat of your majesty,
   the great place of your burning love,
   the altar of forgiveness
      set up by your mercy
      and in which your glory dwells;
we your people and the sheep of your pasture
join our voices
   with those of unnumbered Cherubim
      who praise you
   and of the myriads of seraphim and archangels
      who sing your holiness.
We fall down in worship, to praise
and glorify you forever,
   Lord of all,
      Father, Son, and Holy Spirit.

Your death, O Lord, we commemorate.
Your resurrection we confess.
Your coming we await.

As this bread was once scattered over the hills
    and then was brought together and made one,
so let your Church be brought together from the ends
    of the earth into your Kingdom;
For yours is the glory and the power
    through Jesus Christ forever.

Before Communing

Lord, come to me and cleanse me,
   come to me and heal me,
   come to me and strengthen me;
and grant that having received you,
   I may never be separated from you,
   but may continue yours forever.

Soul of Christ, sanctify me;
Body of Christ, save me;
Blood of Christ, refresh me;
Water from the side of Christ, wash me;
Passion of Christ, strengthen me;
O good Jesus, hear me;
Within your wounds hide me;
Let me not be separated from you;
From the malicious enemy defend me;
In the hour of death call me;
And bid me come to you,
That with the saints I may praise you
   through the ages of eternity

Hear us, O Lord Jesus Christ,
from your dwelling place,
  from the glorious throne of your kingdom,
  and come and cleanse us.
You are seated on high with the Father,
  and you dwell also with us here, although unseen.
By your mighty hand render us worthy to receive
in holy communion
  your spotless body and your precious blood.

☩

Lord, be merciful to me a sinner.

Unite us all who partake of the one bread and the
one cup
  one to another in the communion
  of the Holy Spirit,
and grant that none of us may partake
    of that holy body and blood of Christ
  unto judgment or condemnation
but that we may find mercy and grace
  together with all the saints,
    who throughout the ages have been acceptable
      to you:
    our forebears, the Patriarchs, Prophets, Apos-
      tles,

Preachers, Evangelists, Martyrs, Confessors,
Teachers,
and with all the righteous who have died in the
faith.

✠

Lo, I draw near to the King immortal and our God.

I believe, O Lord, and I confess
that you are the Christ, the Son of the living God,
who came into the world to save sinners,
of whom I am the greatest.
And I believe that this is indeed your most pure body
and your own precious blood.
Wherefore I pray you to have mercy on me and pardon
my offences,
voluntary or involuntary, of word or of deed,
whether committed with knowledge or
in ignorance,
and count me worthy to share without
condemnation
in your all-pure Mysteries
for the remission of sins and for eternal life.
Receive me now, O Son of God, as a communicant
of your Mystical Supper,
for I will not reveal your mystery to your enemies

nor like Judas give you a kiss,
   but like the repentant thief I will say,
      Lord, remember me in your Kingdom.
Let not this participation in your Holy Mysteries
   be to judgment upon me or condemnation,
   but to the healing of soul and body.

O Lord, be merciful to me, a sinner.

✠

We do not presume to come to your table, O Lord,
   trusting in our own righteousness,
   but in your manifold and great mercies.
We are not worthy to gather up the crumbs under
   your table.
But you are the same Lord whose property is always
   to have mercy.
Grant us, therefore, gracious Lord,
   so to eat the flesh of your dear Son Jesus Christ,
   and so to drink his blood,
      that we may evermore dwell in him and he in us.

✠

Remember, O Lord, what you have wrought in us
   and not what we deserve;
and, as you have called us to your service,

make us worthy of our calling;
through Jesus Christ our Lord.

☩

The Master is here and calls for you (See John 11:28).

☩

Here stand the gracious and lovely words, "This is my body, given *for you*." "This is my blood, poured out *for you*, for the forgiveness of sins." . . . Ponder, then, and include yourself personally in the "you" so that he may not speak to you in vain.

In this sacrament he offers us all the treasure he brought from heaven for us. . . .

—Martin Luther

☩

Approach with the fear of God and with faith.

Receive the body of Christ.
Taste the fountain of life.

At the Communion

"My Lord and my God!" (John 20:28)

After Communing

I have found him whom my soul loves;
I will hold him and not let him go.

(See Song of Sol. 3:4)

How awesome is this place!
This is none other than the house of God,
and this is the gate of heaven.

(Gen. 28:17)

GIVE THANKS

For Life,
With Life

After Communing

If you wish to understand the body of Christ,
listen to the words of the Apostle, "You are the body
   of Christ."
If therefore you are the body of Christ
   and his members,
it is the sacrament of yourselves that is set upon the
   Lord's table,
the sacrament of yourselves that you receive.
Be what you receive, and receive what you are.
You hear the words, "The body of Christ,"
   and you answer, "Amen."
Be a member of the body of Christ
   so that your Amen may be honest.

If you have received well, you are that which you
   receive.

                    —St. Augustine

✠

We communicate not only by participating
   and partaking,
but also by being united. . . .
For as the bread consisting of many grains is made
one, so that the grains nowhere appear;
   they exist indeed,
      but their difference is not seen because of their
      union;

so we are joined with each other and with Christ,
there not being one body to nourish you
and another to nourish your neighbor,
but the very same for all.
Wherefore the Apostle adds, "For we all parrtake of
the one bread."
Now if we are all members of the same and all become
the same,
why do we not also show forth the same love
and in this respect also become one?

—St. John Chrysostom

✛

I am no longer my own, but yours.
Put me to what you will, rank me with whom
you will;
Put me to doing, put me to suffering;
Let me be employed for you or laid aside for you;
exalted for you or brought low for you;
Let me be full, let me be empty;
Let me have all things, let me have nothing;
I freely and heartily yield all things to your pleasure
and disposal.
And now, O glorious and blessed God,
Father, Son, and Holy Spirit,
You are mine, and I am yours. So be it.

—John Wesley

Thanksgiving after Communion

We have partaken of the holy, pure, deathless,
   heavenly, life-giving, and awesome Mysteries of
   Christ.
   Let us therefore give thanks to the Lord.

Christ has shown himself among us.
God has made his dwelling place in the midst of us.
The voice of peace has spoken,
   this holy salutation has been made ours,
   enmity has been taken away,
   and love has reached every part.
Lift up your voices
   and with one accord
      bless the holy and undivided Trinity
      to whom the seraphim sing hymns of praise.

Antiphon   The Lord gave them bread from heaven,
            so mortals ate the food of angels.
                                    (Ps. 78:24-25)

Bless the Lord, O my soul,
   and all that is within me, bless his holy name.
Bless the Lord, O my soul,
   and forget not all his benefits.

He forgives all your sins
    and heals all your infirmities;
he redeems your life from the grave
    and crowns you with mercy and lovingkindness;
he satisfies you with good things,
    and your youth is renewed like an eagle's.

$$\text{(Ps. 103:1-5)}$$

Antiphon   The Lord gave them bread from heaven,
            so mortals ate the food of angels.

Let us bless the Father and the Son and the Holy
Spirit—
    praise him and magnify him forever.
All your works praise you, O Lord,
    and your faithful servants bless you (Ps. 145:10).
Not to us, O Lord, not to us,
    but to your name give glory (Ps. 115:1).
Lord hear my prayer,
    and let my cry come before you (Ps. 102:1).

☩

Let our mouths be filled with your praise, O Lord,
    so that we may extol your glory;
for you have deigned to make us partakers
    of your holy, divine, immortal, and life-giving
    Mysteries.
Keep us in your holiness
    so that all the day long
    we may remember your righteousness
      Alleluia. Alleluia. Alleluia.

✝

O Christ, Lamb of God pure and holy,
    O Wisdom, Word, and Power of God,
    grant that we may more perfectly partake of you
      in the days which know no ending
      in your Kingdom.

✝

A Prayer of Thomas Aquinas

I give you thanks, O Lord, holy Father,
everlasting God.
In your great mercy,
    and not because of my own merits,
    you have fed me,
    a sinner and your unworthy servant,

with the precious Body and Blood of your Son,
  our Lord Jesus Christ.
I pray that this Holy Communion
  may not serve as my judgment and condemnation
  but as my forgiveness and salvation.
Make it to me my armor of faith,
  my shield of good purpose.
May it root out in me all vice and evil desires,
    increase my love and patience,
    humility and obedience,
    and every virtue.
Make it a firm defence against the wiles
    of all my enemies,
  seen and unseen,
  while restraining all evil impulses of flesh and spirit.
May it help me to cleave to you,
  the one true God,
  and bring me a blessed death when you call.
I beseech you to bring me, a sinner,
  to that ineffable feast where,
  with your Son and the Holy Spirit,
  you are the true light of your holy ones,
    their flawless blessedness,
    everlasting joy,
    and perfect happiness;
  through Christ our Lord.

He has showed you, O mortal, what is good;
   and what does the Lord require of you
but to do justice, and to love kindness,
   and to walk humbly with your God?

(Mic. 6:8)

To him who loves us
   and has freed us from our sins by his blood
   and made us a kingdom,
   priests to his God and Father,
to him be glory and dominion
   forever and ever, Amen.

(Rev. 1:5-6)

GO IN PEACE

And Serve
The Lord

When you reflect after Communion, "What have I done today?" say to yourself, "I have done more than on any busiest day of the week. I have yielded myself to take part with the Church in Christ's finished Act of Redemption, which is greater than the making of the world."

—P. T. Forsyth

✠

O Lord, you have called us to be your witnesses.
Cleanse us from all unbelief and sloth and fill us with hope and zeal,
that we may do your work,
    and bear your cross,
    and bide your time,
    and see your glory.

✠

Strengthen for service, Lord, the hands
  That holy things have taken;
Let ears that now have heard thy songs
  To clamor never waken.

Lord, may the tongues which "Holy" sang
  Keep free from all deceiving;
The eyes which saw thy love be bright,
  Thy blessed hope perceiving.

The feet that tread thy hallowed courts
  From light do thou not banish;
The bodies by thy spirit fed
  With thy new life replenish.

                 —Liturgy of Malabar

After the Service

Finished and perfected, O Christ our God,
   so far as in us lies,
is the Mystery which you have ordained.
We have made the memorial of your death,
we have seen the symbol of your resurrection,
we have been enriched with your inexhaustible
   bounty
     and filled with your undying life;
and of this count us worthy in the world to come.

☩

Going on from strength to strength,
   and having fulfilled all the divine service in your
   temple,
now we ask you, O Lord our God,
   make us worthy of perfect lovingkindness,
   make our path straight,
   root us in your fear,
   and make us worthy of your heavenly kingdom
     in Jesus Christ our Lord,
       with whom you are blessed,
     together with your all-holy and life-creating
     Spirit,
       now and always and unto ages of ages.

☩

Thus a Christian life is nothing else than a daily baptism, once begun and ever continued. For we must keep at it incessantly, always purging out whatever pertains to the old Adam, so that whatever belongs to the new may come forth.

Therefore let everybody regard our baptism as the daily garment which we are to wear all the time. . . . If we wish to be Christians, we must practice the work that makes us Christians.

—Martin Luther

✠

Let us love one another
so that with one mind
we may glorify the Father and the Son and the
Holy Spirit,
the Trinity one in essence and undivided.

The church doors, which closed after us when we entered the house of the church, now open for us upon the world which awaits our service. We go out from our worship with our eyes newly opened to the beauty of the physical world which bears the Creator's revelation to us.

The earth is the Lord's and all that is in it,
    the world and all who dwell therein.

(Ps. 24:1)

He who sat upon the throne said,
    "Behold, I make all things new."

(Rev. 21:5)

Sources

Psalm quotations are from the *Standard Book of Common Prayer*, copyright © 1977 by Charles Mortimer Guilbert as custodian.

p. 4   "O sacred feast . . . ," *O sacrum convivium*, is the antiphon to the Magnificat at the second vespers of Corpus Christi to Thomas Aquinas. Translation by Philip H. Pfatteicher.

p. 6   Quotation by Bishop Bo Giertz is from a sermon at the 800th anniversary of the Archdiocese of Uppsala, June 1964. Quoted in *Minister's Information Service*, April 1965. Quotation by Martin Luther is from *The Blessed Sacrament of the Holy and True Body of Christ*, in *Luther's Works*, vol. 35, pp. 53, 67. Copyright 1960 by Fortress Press. Used by permission of the publisher.

pp. 8-16   Adaptation of the liturgy of the Syrian Jacobites is from *The Treasury of Devotion*, ed. T. T. Carter (Nashville: Thomas Nelson, 1938), and is used by permission.

p. 17   "Lord God, you taught . . ." is from *Lutheran Book of Worship*, Minister's Edition, copyright © 1978, pp. 110-111.

p. 20   "Eternal God . . ." is from the Gelasian sacramentary. Adapted with permission from *The Cuddesdon College Office Book*, copyright © 1961, Oxford University Press. "Jesus, Master . . ." is a Mozarabic prayer reprinted from *Oremus* by P. Strodach (Augsburg Publishing House), p. 154. "Come, Lord Jesus . . ." is from *Book of Prayers for All Churchmen* (Cambridge: Society of St. John the Evangelist, 1944), p. 21.

p. 21   "O Lord, forgive the sins . . ." is from the liturgy of Malabar. Translation by P. Pfatteicher. "Lord God of all ages . . ." is from the *Standard Book of Common Prayer*, copyright © 1977 by Charles Mortimer Guilbert as custodian.

p. 22   "Come, Lord Jesus . . ." is part of the Mozarabic liturgy, from Luke 24:36. "As watchmen wait . . ." is based on Psalm 130:6. "Reveal yourself to us . . ." is from *Lutheran Book of Worship*, Minister's Edition, copyright © 1978, p. 29.

pp. 23-25   Adaptation of the liturgy of the Syrian Jacobites is from *The Cuddesdon College Office Book*, pp. 157-159, copyright © 1961 Oxford University Press. Used by permission.

p. 26   "Holy Lord . . ." is from the asperges of the Roman Mass. Translation from the Latin by P. Pfatteicher.

p. 31   "Grant, O Lord . . ." is from *Oremus*, p. 154. "Wisdom . . ." is from the liturgy of St. John Chrysostom. Translation by P. Pfatteicher.

p. 32   "When the Gospel is read . . ." is from *Apostolic Constitutions* II.7.57. Adaptation by P. Pfatteicher.

p. 33   "Remember all your creation . . ." is from *Preces Privatae* by Lancelot Andrewes, translated by F. E. Brightman, 1903. Revised by P. Pfatteicher.

p. 37   "Let us who mystically . . ." is from the liturgy of St. John Chrysostom. Translation by P. Pfatteicher. "Before the glorious throne . . ." is adapted by P. Pfatteicher from the translation by Donald Attwater, *Eastern Catholic Worship* (New York: Devin-Adair Co., 1945). "Your death, O Lord, we commemorate . . ." is adapted by P. Pfatteicher from the *Book of Common Worship* of the Church of South India (Oxford: Oxford, 1963). "As this bread was once scattered . . ." is from the *Didache*. Translation by P. Pfatteicher.

p. 39   "Lord, come to me and cleanse me . . ." is used by permission from *The Treasury of Devotion*, ed. T. T. Carter (Nashville: Thomas Nelson, 1938), p. 70.

pp. 39-42   "Hear us, O Lord Jesus Christ . . . ," "Unite us all who partake . . . ," "Lo, I draw near . . . ," and "I believe, O Lord . . . ," are from the liturgy of St. John Chrysostom. Translation by P. Pfatteicher.

p. 56   "Finished and perfected . . ." is from the liturgy of St. Basil. "Going from strength to strength . . ." is from the liturgy of St. James.

p. 57   "Thus a Christian life . . ." is from *Luther's Large Catechism,* in *The Book of Concord.* Copyright 1959 by Fortress Press. Used by permission of the publisher. "Let us love . . ." is from the liturgy of St. John Chrysostom. Translation by P. Pfatteicher.